Audio Access Included

Christmas Carols
for Easy Classical Guitar

Arranged by
Mark Phillips

PLAYBACK+
Speed • Pitch • Balance • Loop

To access audio visit:
www.halleonard.com/mylibrary

Enter Code
3173-6364-5464-9335

Cherry Lane Music Company
Director of Publications/Project Editor: Mark Phillips
Project Coordinator: Rebecca Skidmore

ISBN 978-1-60378-248-7

Visit Hal Leonard Online at
www.halleonard.com

Contents

Angels We Have Heard on High

Traditional French Carol

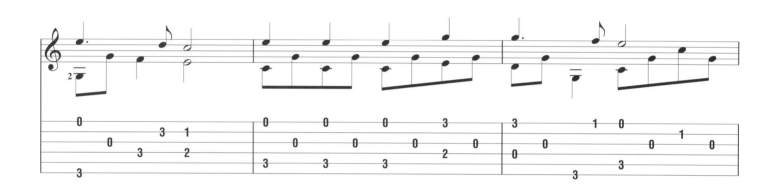

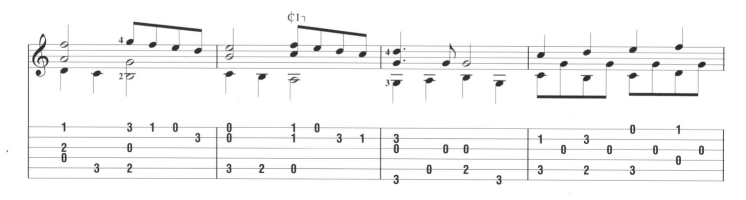

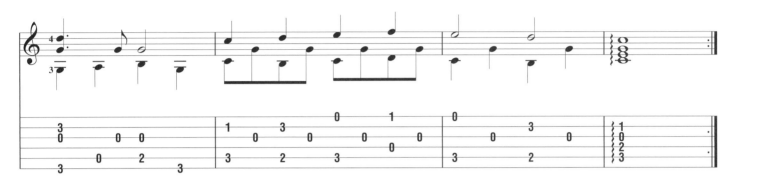

Ave Maria

Franz Schubert

Slowly, in 2

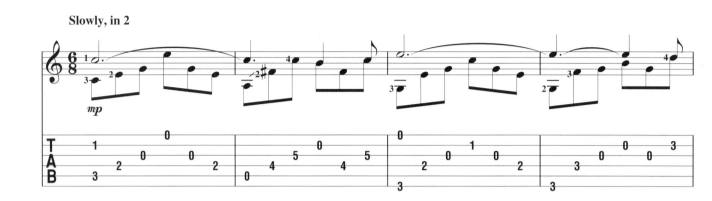

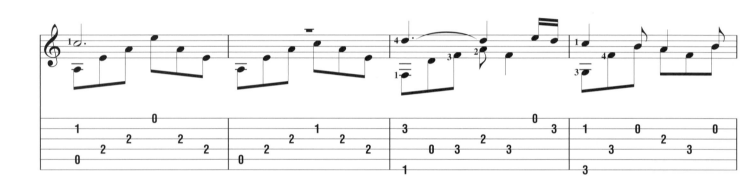

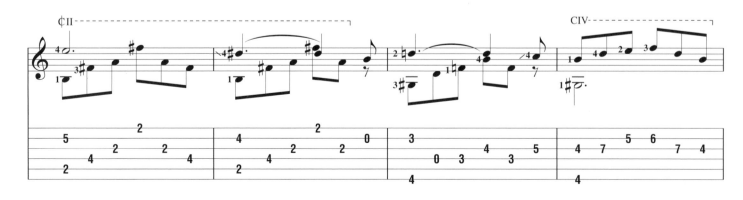

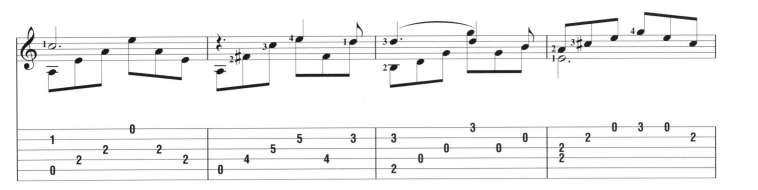

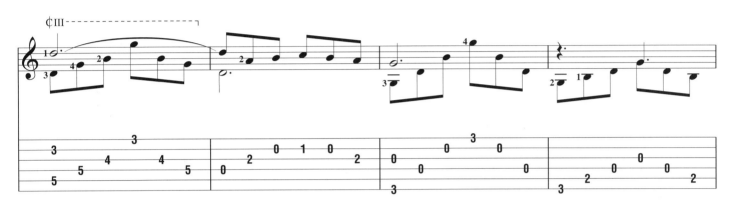

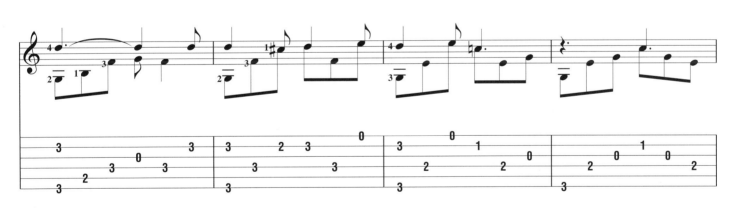

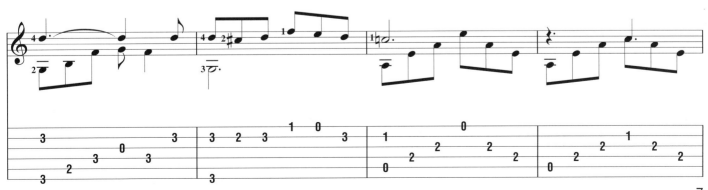

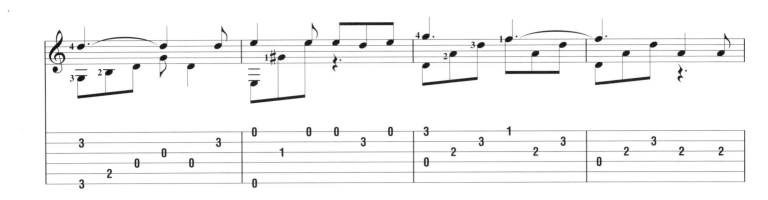

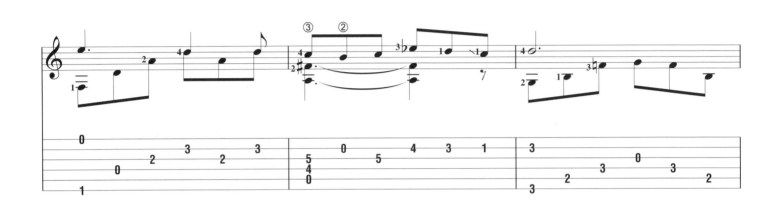

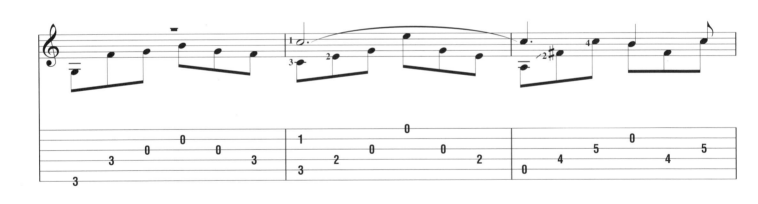

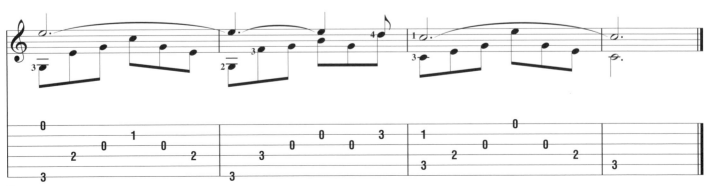

Away in a Manger

Words by John T. McFarland
Music by William J. Kirkpatrick

Deck the Halls

Traditional Welsh Carol

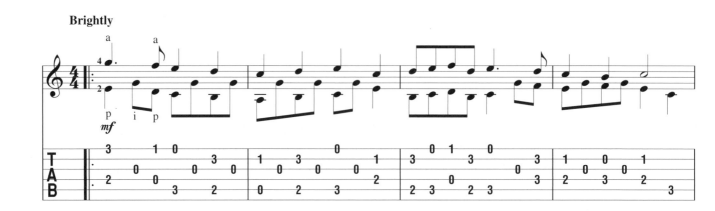

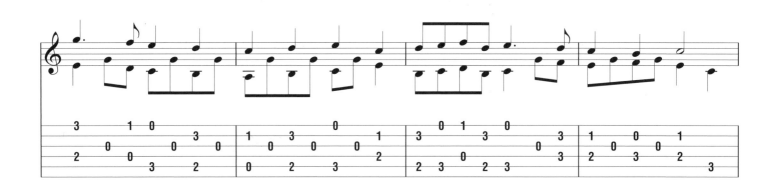

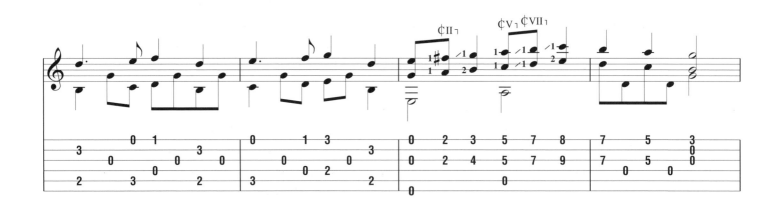

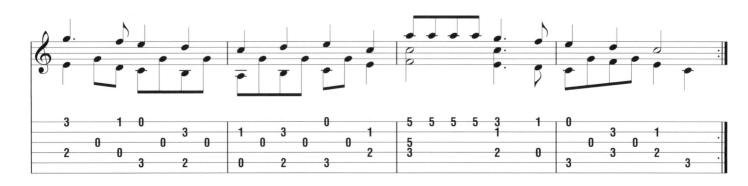

The First Noël

17th Century English Carol

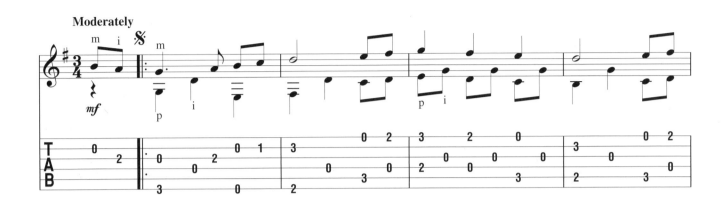

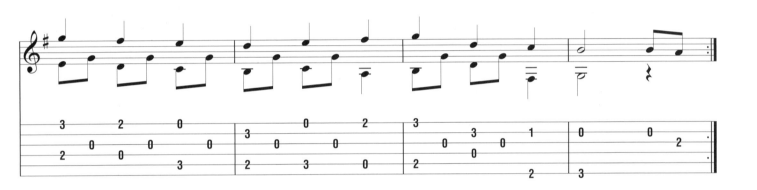

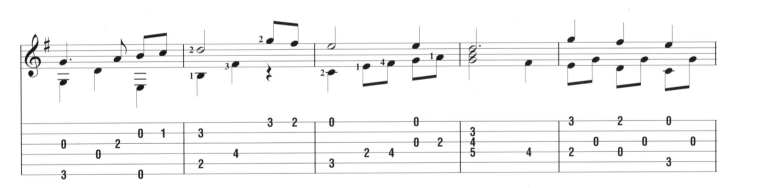

To Coda ⊕   *D.S. (with repeat) al Coda*   ⊕ **Coda**

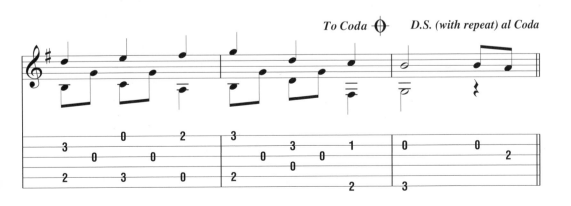

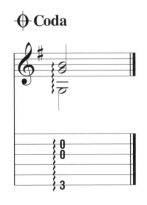

God Rest Ye Merry, Gentlemen

19th Century English Carol

Moderately fast

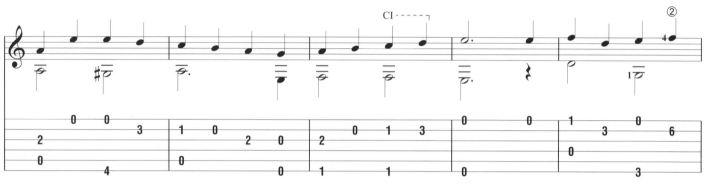

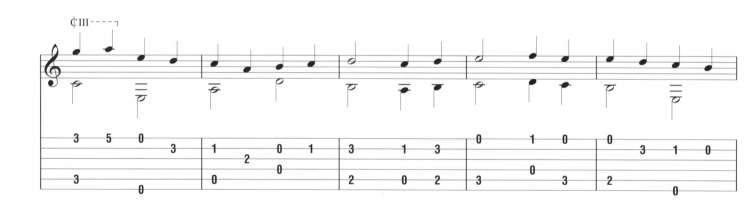

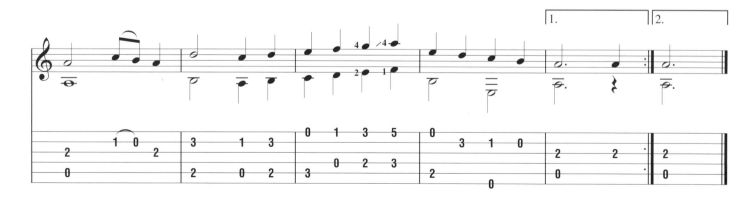

Hark! The Herald Angels Sing

Words by Charles Wesley
Music by Felix Mendelssohn-Bartholdy

It Came upon the Midnight Clear

Words by Edmund H. Sears
Traditional English Melody

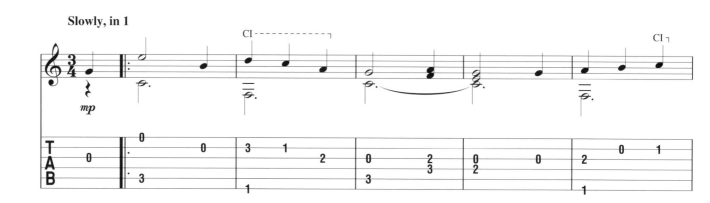

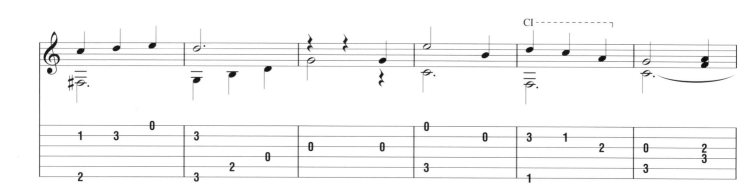

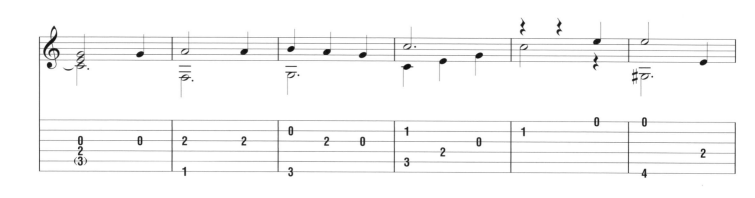

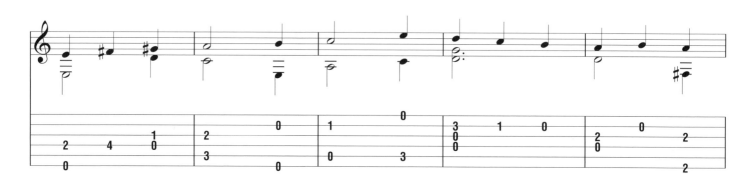

Jesu, Joy of Man's Desiring

Johann Sebastian Bach

Moderately slow

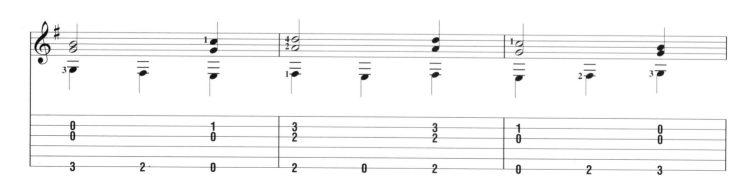

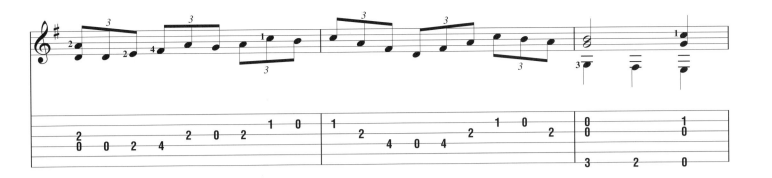

D.S. al Fine

Jingle Bells

Words and Music by J. Pierpont

Moderately bright

Joy to the World

Words by Isaac Watts
Music by George Frideric Handel

Brightly, majestically

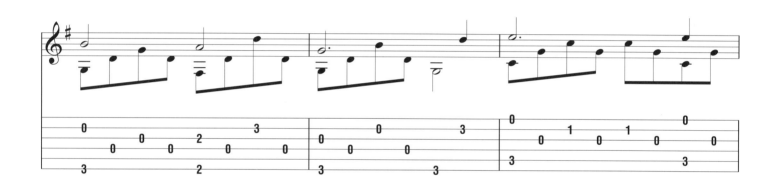

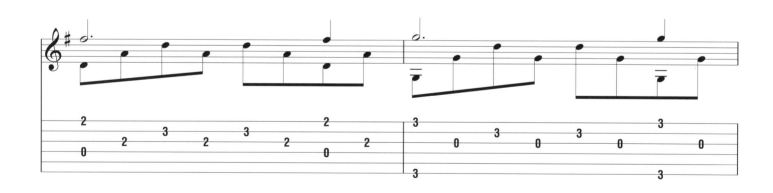

O Come, All Ye Faithful
(Adeste Fideles)

Music by John Francis Wade

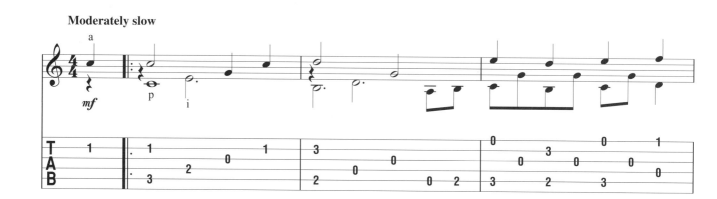

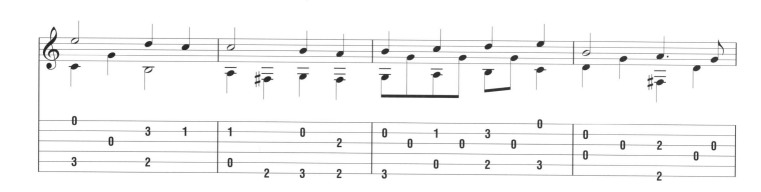

O Christmas Tree

Traditional German Carol

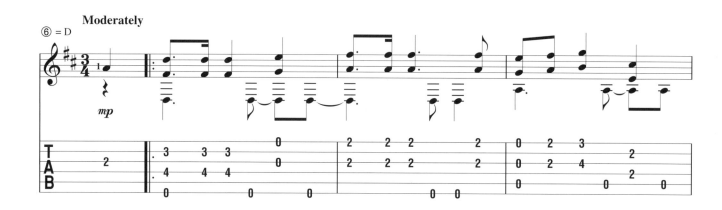

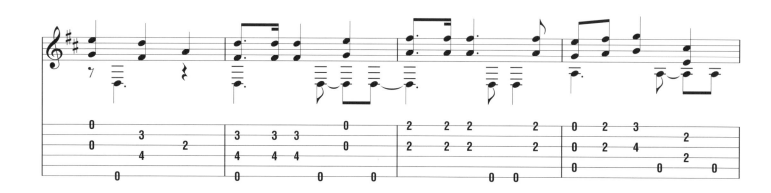

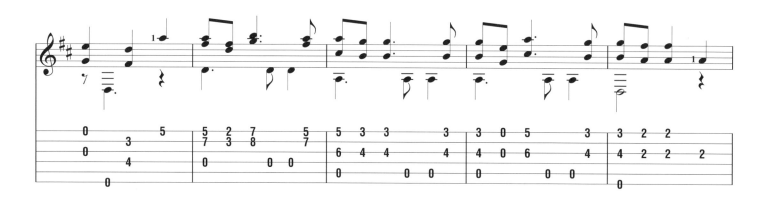

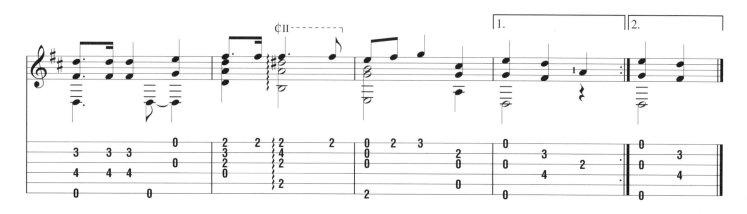

O Come, O Come, Emmanuel

15th Century French Melody

O Holy Night

Music by Adolphe Adam

Moderately slow, in 2

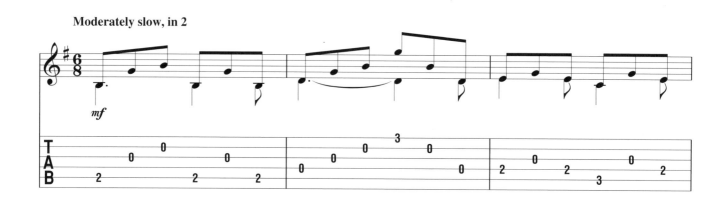

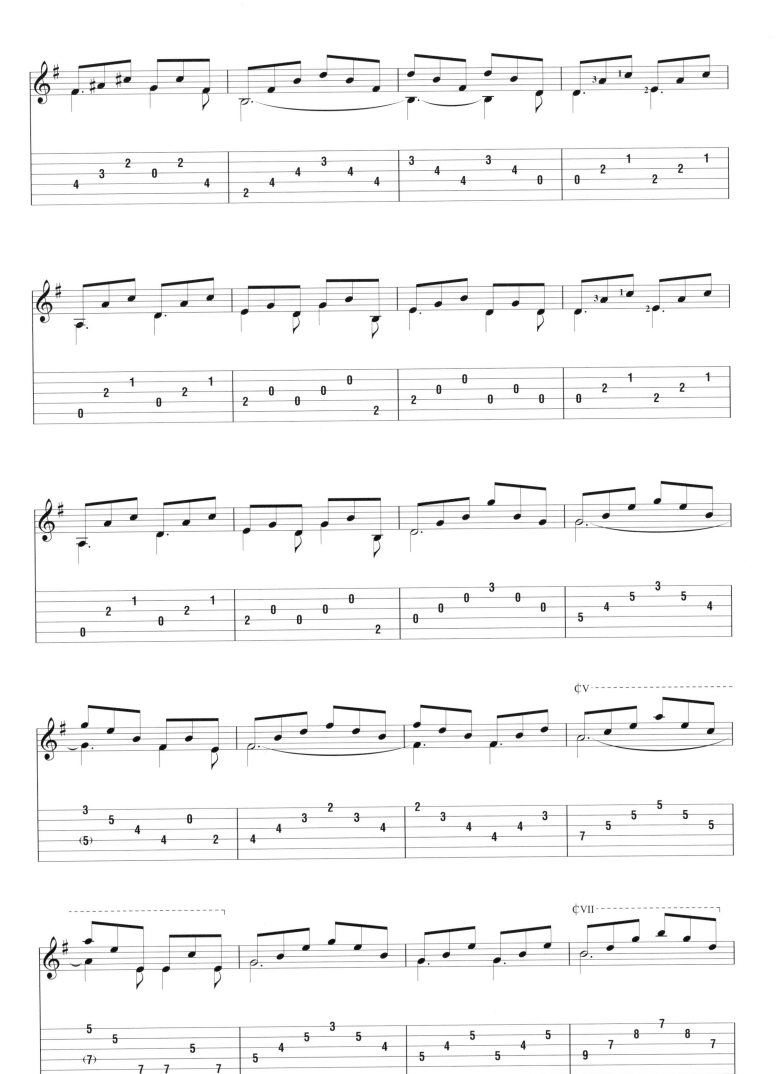

27

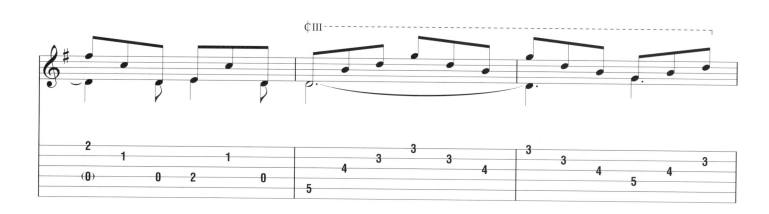

O Little Town of Bethlehem

Words by Phillips Brooks
Music based on Traditional English Melody

Moderately

Once in Royal David's City

Words by Cecil F. Alexander
Music by Henry J. Gauntlett

Moderately

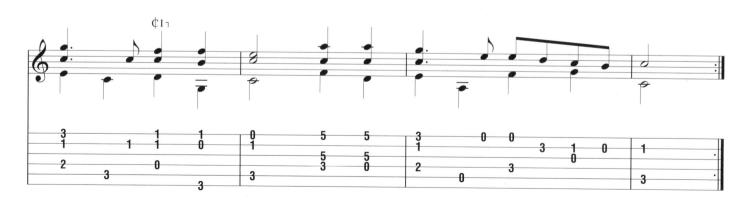

The Twelve Days of Christmas

Traditional English Carol

Moderately

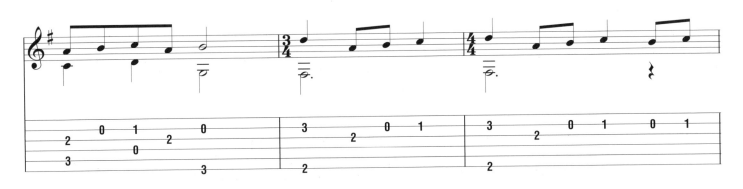

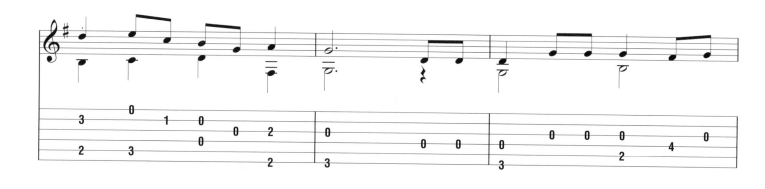

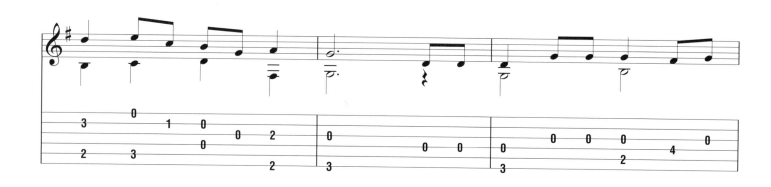

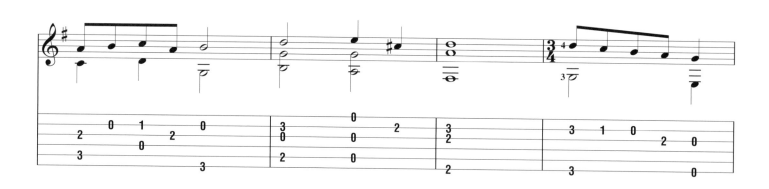

*This measure to be repeated one additional time
for each repeat of the **B** section.

**For repeats

Last time

Play **B section as often as desired,
up to a maximum of seven times.

Silent Night

Words by Joseph Mohr
Music by Franz X. Gruber

Moderately

We Three Kings of Orient Are

Words and Music by John H. Hopkins, Jr.

Slowly, in 1

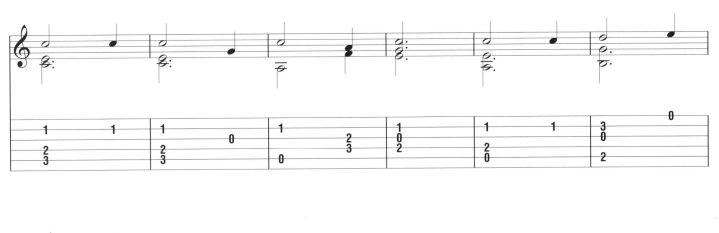

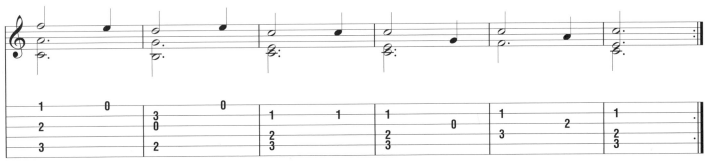

We Wish You a Merry Christmas

Traditional English Folksong

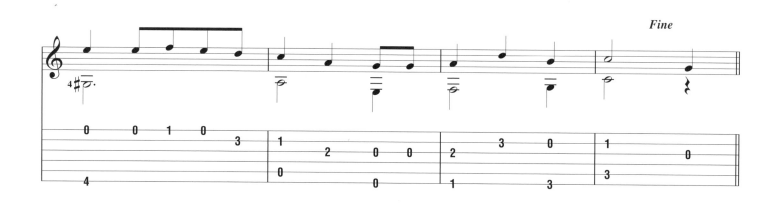

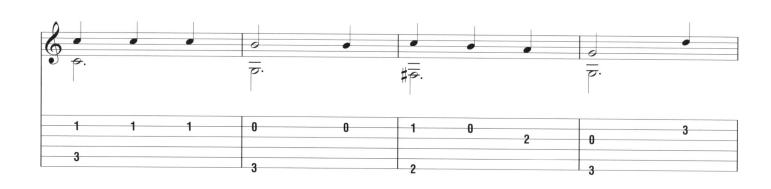

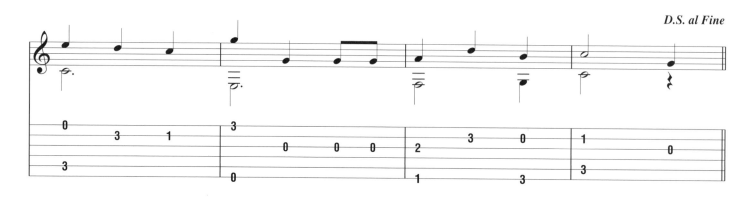

What Child Is This?

16th Century English Melody

Moderately slow, in 2

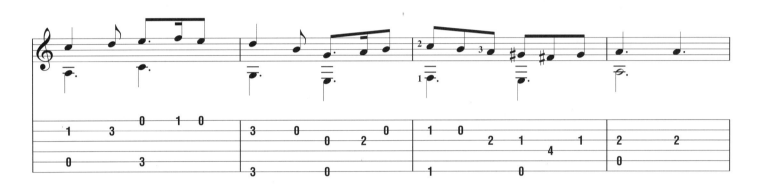

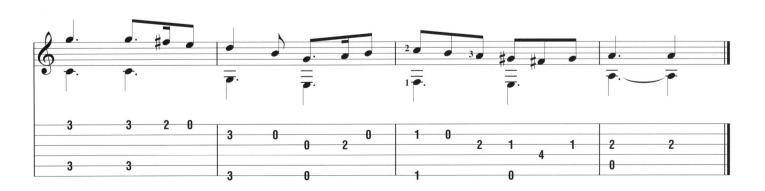

RECORDED VERSIONS®
The Best Note-For-Note Transcriptions Available

AUTHENTIC TRANSCRIPTIONS WITH NOTES AND TABLATURE

00690603	Aerosmith – O Yeah! Ultimate Hits	$29.99
00690178	Alice in Chains – Acoustic	$22.99
00694865	Alice in Chains – Dirt	$19.99
00694925	Alice in Chains – Jar of Flies/Sap	$19.99
00691091	Alice Cooper – Best of	$24.99
00690958	Duane Allman – Guitar Anthology	$29.99
00694932	Allman Brothers Band – Volume 1	$29.99
00694933	Allman Brothers Band – Volume 2	$27.99
00694934	Allman Brothers Band – Volume 3	$29.99
00690945	Alter Bridge – Blackbird	$24.99
00123558	Arctic Monkeys – AM	$24.99
00214869	Avenged Sevenfold – Best of 2005-2013	$29.99
00690489	Beatles – 1	$24.99
00694929	Beatles – 1962-1966	$27.99
00694930	Beatles – 1967-1970	$29.99
00694880	Beatles – Abbey Road	$19.99
00694832	Beatles – Acoustic Guitar	$27.99
00690110	Beatles – White Album (Book 1)	$19.99
00692385	Chuck Berry	$24.99
00147787	Black Crowes – Best of	$24.99
00690149	Black Sabbath	$19.99
00690901	Black Sabbath – Best of	$22.99
00691010	Black Sabbath – Heaven and Hell	$24.99
00690148	Black Sabbath – Master of Reality	$19.99
00690142	Black Sabbath – Paranoid	$19.99
00148544	Michael Bloomfield – Guitar Anthology	$24.99
00158600	Joe Bonamassa – Blues of Desperation	$24.99
00198117	Joe Bonamassa – Muddy Wolf at Red Rocks	$24.99
00283540	Joe Bonamassa – Redemption	$24.99
00358863	Joe Bonamassa – Royal Tea	$24.99
00690913	Boston	$22.99
00690491	David Bowie – Best of	$22.99
00286503	Big Bill Broonzy – Guitar Collection	$19.99
00690261	The Carter Family Collection	$19.99
00691079	Johnny Cash – Best of	$24.99
00690936	Eric Clapton – Complete Clapton	$34.99
00694869	Eric Clapton – Unplugged	$24.99
00124873	Eric Clapton – Unplugged (Deluxe)	$29.99
00138731	Eric Clapton & Friends – The Breeze	$24.99
00139967	Coheed & Cambria – In Keeping Secrets of Silent Earth: 3	$24.99
00141704	Jesse Cook – Works, Vol. 1	$19.99
00288787	Creed – Greatest Hits	$22.99
00690819	Creedence Clearwater Revival	$27.99
00690648	Jim Croce – Very Best of	$19.99
00690572	Steve Cropper – Soul Man	$22.99
00690613	Crosby, Stills & Nash – Best of	$29.99
00690784	Def Leppard – Best of	$24.99
00694831	Derek and the Dominos – Layla & Other Assorted Love Songs	$24.99
00291164	Dream Theater – Distance Over Time	$24.99
00278631	Eagles – Greatest Hits 1971-1975	$22.99
00278632	Eagles – Very Best of	$39.99
00690515	Extreme II – Pornograffiti	$24.99
00150257	John Fahey – Guitar Anthology	$24.99
00690664	Fleetwood Mac – Best of	$24.99
00691024	Foo Fighters – Greatest Hits	$24.99
00120220	Robben Ford – Guitar Anthology	$29.99
00295410	Rory Gallagher – Blues	$24.99
00139460	Grateful Dead – Guitar Anthology	$34.99
00691190	Peter Green – Best of	$24.99

00287517	Greta Van Fleet – Anthem of the Peaceful Army	$22.99
00287515	Greta Van Fleet – From the Fires	$19.99
00694798	George Harrison – Anthology	$24.99
00692930	Jimi Hendrix – Are You Experienced?	$29.99
00692931	Jimi Hendrix – Axis: Bold As Love	$24.99
00690304	Jimi Hendrix – Band of Gypsys	$27.99
00694944	Jimi Hendrix – Blues	$29.99
00692932	Jimi Hendrix – Electric Ladyland	$27.99
00660029	Buddy Holly – Best of	$24.99
00200446	Iron Maiden – Guitar Tab	$34.99
00694912	Eric Johnson – Ah Via Musicom	$24.99
00690271	Robert Johnson – Transcriptions	$27.99
00690427	Judas Priest – Best of	$24.99
00690492	B.B. King – Anthology	$29.99
00130447	B.B. King – Live at the Regal	$19.99
00690134	Freddie King – Collection	$22.99
00327968	Marcus King – El Dorado	$22.99
00690157	Kiss – Alive	$19.99
00690356	Kiss – Alive II	$24.99
00291163	Kiss – Very Best of	$24.99
00345767	Greg Koch – Best of	$29.99
00690377	Kris Kristofferson – Guitar Collection	$22.99
00690834	Lamb of God – Ashes of the Wake	$24.99
00690525	George Lynch – Best of	$29.99
00690955	Lynyrd Skynyrd – All-Time Greatest Hits	$24.99
00694954	Lynyrd Skynyrd – New Best of	$24.99
00690577	Yngwie Malmsteen – Anthology	$29.99
00694896	John Mayall with Eric Clapton – Blues Breakers	$19.99
00694952	Megadeth – Countdown to Extinction	$24.99
00276065	Megadeth – Greatest Hits: Back to the Start	$27.99
00694951	Megadeth – Rust in Peace	$27.99
00690011	Megadeth – Youthanasia	$24.99
00209876	Metallica – Hardwired to Self-Destruct	$24.99
00690646	Pat Metheny – One Quiet Night	$24.99
00102591	Wes Montgomery – Guitar Anthology	$27.99
00691092	Gary Moore – Best of	$27.99
00694802	Gary Moore – Still Got the Blues	$24.99
00355456	Alanis Morisette – Jagged Little Pill	$22.99
00690611	Nirvana	$24.99
00694913	Nirvana – In Utero	$22.99
00694883	Nirvana – Nevermind	$19.99
00690026	Nirvana – Unplugged in New York	$19.99
00265439	Nothing More – Tab Collection	$24.99
00243349	Opeth – Best of	$22.99
00690499	Tom Petty – Definitive Guitar Collection	$24.99
00121933	Pink Floyd – Acoustic Guitar Collection	$27.99
00690428	Pink Floyd – Dark Side of the Moon	$22.99
00244637	Pink Floyd – Guitar Anthology	$24.99
00239799	Pink Floyd – The Wall	$27.99
00690789	Poison – Best of	$22.99
00690925	Prince – Very Best of	$24.99
00690003	Queen – Classic Queen	$24.99
00694975	Queen – Greatest Hits	$25.99
00694910	Rage Against the Machine	$24.99
00119834	Rage Against the Machine – Guitar Anthology	$24.99
00690426	Ratt – Best of	$24.99
00690055	Red Hot Chili Peppers – Blood Sugar Sex Magik	$19.99

00690379	Red Hot Chili Peppers – Californication	$22.99
00690673	Red Hot Chili Peppers – Greatest Hits	$24.99
00690852	Red Hot Chili Peppers – Stadium Arcadium	$29.99
00690511	Django Reinhardt – Definitive Collection	$24.99
00690014	Rolling Stones – Exile on Main Street	$24.99
00690631	Rolling Stones – Guitar Anthology	$34.99
00323854	Rush – The Spirit of Radio: Greatest Hits, 1974-1987	$22.99
00173534	Santana – Guitar Anthology	$29.99
00276350	Joe Satriani – What Happens Next	$24.99
00690566	Scorpions – Best of	$24.99
00690604	Bob Seger – Guitar Collection	$24.99
00234543	Ed Sheeran – Divide*	$19.99
00691114	Slash – Guitar Anthology	$34.99
00690813	Slayer – Guitar Collection	$24.99
00690419	Slipknot	$22.99
00316982	Smashing Pumpkins – Greatest Hits	$24.99
00690912	Soundgarden – Guitar Anthology	$24.99
00120004	Steely Dan – Best of	$27.99
00322564	Stone Temple Pilots – Thank You	$22.99
00690520	Styx – Guitar Collection	$22.99
00120081	Sublime	$22.99
00690531	System of a Down – Toxicity	$19.99
00694824	James Taylor – Best of	$19.99
00694887	Thin Lizzy – Best of	$22.99
00253237	Trivium – Guitar Tab Anthology	$24.99
00690683	Robin Trower – Bridge of Sighs	$19.99
00156024	Steve Vai – Guitar Anthology	$39.99
00660137	Steve Vai – Passion & Warfare	$29.99
00295076	Van Halen – 30 Classics	$29.99
00690024	Stevie Ray Vaughan – Couldn't Stand the Weather	$22.99
00660058	Stevie Ray Vaughan – Lightnin' Blues 1983-1987	$29.99
00217455	Stevie Ray Vaughan – Plays Slow Blues	$24.99
00694835	Stevie Ray Vaughan – The Sky Is Crying	$24.99
00690015	Stevie Ray Vaughan – Texas Flood	$22.99
00694789	Muddy Waters – Deep Blues	$27.99
00152161	Doc Watson – Guitar Anthology	$24.99
00690071	Weezer (The Blue Album)	$22.99
00237811	White Stripes – Greatest Hits	$24.99
00117511	Whitesnake – Guitar Collection	$24.99
00122303	Yes – Guitar Collection	$24.99
00690443	Frank Zappa – Hot Rats	$22.99
00121684	ZZ Top – Early Classics	$27.99
00690589	ZZ Top – Guitar Anthology	$24.99

COMPLETE SERIES LIST ONLINE!

HAL•LEONARD®
www.halleonard.com

Prices and availability subject to change without notice.
*Tab transcriptions only.

0622
272